# The Book of Puzzles and Enigmas

This edition published in 2016 by
CHARTWELL BOOKS
an imprint of Book Sales
a division of Quarto Publishing Group USA Inc.
142 West 36th Street, 4th Floor
New York, New York 10018
USA

English translation by Tom Clegg

Letters 'P' and 'E' illustrations on front cover
and title page © 1999 Pepin van Roojen

ISBN 978-0-7858-3454-0

Printed in China

# The Book of Puzzles and Enigmas

Fabrice Mazza
Sylvain Lhullier
Illustrations by Ivan Sigg

CHARTWELL
BOOKS

# CONTENTS

|  | Riddle | Solution |
|---|---|---|

# NTRODUCTION - TO THE READER

Is there anyone out there who doesn't enjoy challenging their friends' minds with a brain-teasing enigma - especially one that may leave them completely flummoxed?

The tradition of enigmas dates back millennia. They have been passed on, transformed and enriched over the years in countless homes, as well as through myths, literature and in our own times, the Internet.

I have selected the best and most amusing enigmas of a certain type, ones that require inventiveness, shrewdness and wisdom to solve.

Because the pleasure of a good enigma lies in seeking... but also in finding - and finding on your own - the path to the solution. No two people arrive at the solution in the same way, and therein lies the interest in sharing these puzzles with friends. So I urge you, dear reader, not to look at the answers except in case of imminent cerebral meltdown.

This book is intended to carry on the tradition of enigmas: now it is up to you to pass them on, transform them and further enrich them.

Happy reading, and happy hunting!

Fabrice Mazza

# BRAIN-TEASER

Can you place the five letters A, B, C, D, and E within this square so that no letter is repeated in the same row, or in the same column, or diagonally?

Solution on page 90

 AKE 24 WITH 5, 5, 5 AND 1

How do you get 24 by using each of the numbers 5, 5, 5, and 1? The only operations allowed are addition, subtraction, multiplication and division.

OGICAL SERIES 1

Continue this series:

$$o \; t \; t \; f \; f \; s \; s$$

EAR

Approach and then draw back from the figure opposite, keeping your eyes fixed on the central point. What happens when you do this?

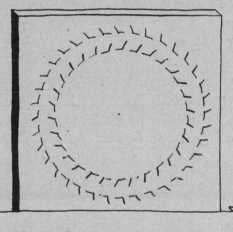

OGICAL SERIES 2

Continue this series:

# EOEREX...

Solution on page 94

 UBTRACTION

How many times can you subtract 6 from 36?

$$36$$
$$- 6$$

Solution on page 95

 RAGONFLY

Tristan and Isolde are separated by 100 furlongs.
  They decide to meet, travelling in sedan chairs
that are borne by porters at a speed of 10 furlongs
per hour.

  A dragonfly, whose speed is 150 furlongs per
hour, then starts an uninterrupted journey back
and forth between the two sedan chairs.

  What distance has it travelled at the moment
when the two lovers finally meet?

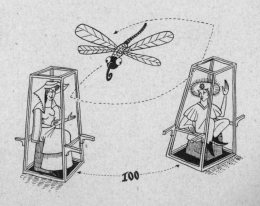

# PATHS

Draw lines linking dwellings 1 to 1, 2 to 2 and 3 to 3, without crossing lines or going outside the frame of this picture.

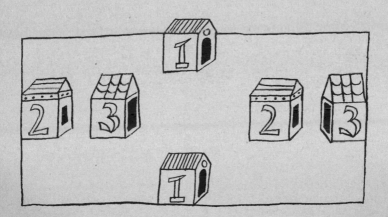

Solution on page 97

# ALLEGIANCE

Robin Hood captures two knights, Sir Thomas and Sir Robert, in Sherwood Forest.

One of them has pledged allegiance to Prince John, the other to King Richard.

When the thief asks them to whom they owe allegiance, Sir Thomas declares, 'I am the bondsman of Prince John,' while Sir Robert says, 'I am the bondsman of King Richard.'

Friar Tuck, who knows both men, affirms that at least one of the pair is lying.

How can Robin Hood determine the truth?

Solution on page 98

 EHIND BARS

When the torches in the corridor are extinguished, what does the prisoner see on the bars of his cell door?

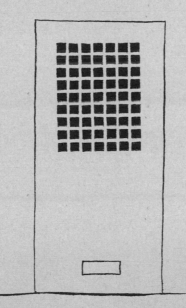

Solution on page 99

# INKWELL

An inkwell and quill costs 11 shillings. The inkwell is worth 10 shillings more than the quill. How much is the inkwell, and how much is the quill?

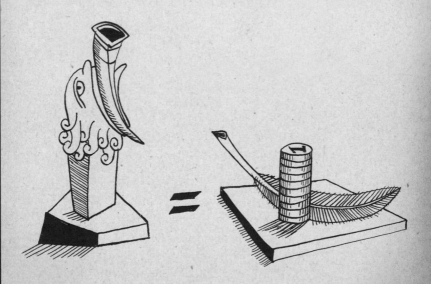

Solution on page 100

# OOL STOCKINGS

Lady Brunehaut is untidy: all of her wool stockings (ten black stockings, eight red stockings, and six white stockings) are mixed together in a chest. She wants to take out a matched pair, but it's dark and the candles have gone out in her chamber.

What is the minimum number of stockings that Lady Brunehaut must remove from the chest to be certain of having two stockings of the same colour?

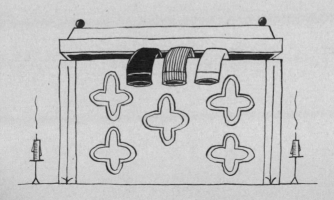

Solution on page 101

ASTIME

The duke of Clarence's cook is preparing a pheasant that his master has brought back from the hunt. He wants to accompany it with a wine sauce that needs to be reduced over exctly 9 minutes.

He has two hourglasses, a big one allowing him to time 7 minutes, and a little one allowing him to measure 4 minutes.

What should he do to time the 9 minutes?

Solution on page 102

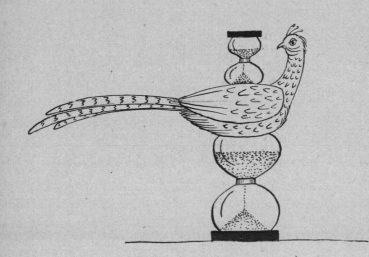

# A T THE MARKET

Lady Ermangarde is extravagant.

At the market, she has spent all she had in her purse at five different traders' shops. At each new shop, she spent 10 shillings more than half of what she had when she entered the establishment.

How much did she have in her purse when she started?

Solution on page 103

# PALINDROME

A knight has ridden 15951 furlongs since he has been in the service of Pepin the Short. He notices that this number is a palindrome (it reads the same from left to right as it does from right to left).

He rides on, and two hours later the total number of furlongs he has travelled is once again a palindrome. How fast is he riding?

Solution on page 104

 RIDGE CROSSING

The bridgekeeper is a terrifying ghoul who appears every 17 minutes. Four people must cross this bridge. Each of them walks at a given maximum speed.

Let us call A the person who can cross the bridge in 1 minute, B the person who can cross in 2 minutes, C the one who needs 5 minutes, and D the laggard who requires 10 minutes.

These four people only have one torch between them, and it is impossible to cross the bridge without this torch.

The bridge can only bear the weight of two people. In which order should they make their crossing?

Solution on page 105

# BALL

Two peasant boys are playing with a ball made of wicker. One of them drops the ball into a cylindrical hole sunk 12 ins deep into the ground. The hole's diameter is a fraction of an inch greater than that of the ball. How can this clumsy boy recover the ball, knowing that the only objects available to him are:

- a sling,
- a horse's hoof,
- an embroidering needle,
- a bucket.

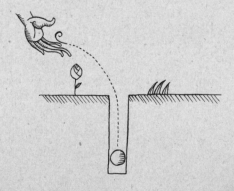

Solution on page 106

# FEBRUARY 29

The son of Lady Gertrude and Sir Baldwin was born on a Monday, February 29. How old will he be the next time his birthday falls on a Monday?

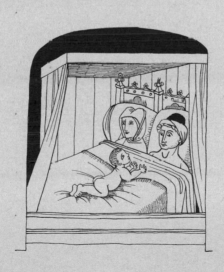

Solution on page 107

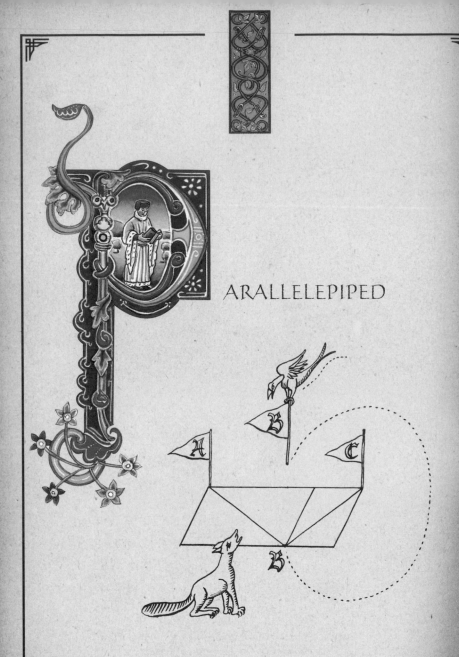

# PARALLELEPIPED

Is segment AB longer than segment BC?

Solution on page 108

# ONG RECTANGLE BECOMES SQUARE

Here is a rectangular parchment whose length (L) measures 5 and width (w) measures 1.

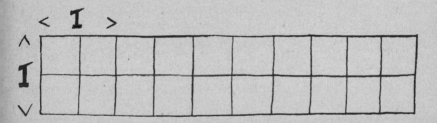

(In the diagram, the scale is 1 : 2)

How can you cut up this parchment in order to make a square with the same surface area, using the pieces?

Solution on page 109

# CYCLING RACE

During a Draisine race, Roland passes the rider in second place, then, as he approaches the finishing line, he is himself passed by two rivals on their wooden push bikes. In what place does he finish?

Solution on page 110

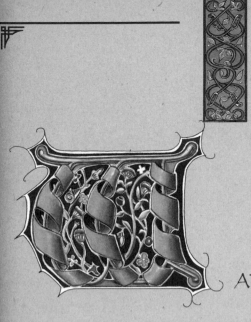

# ATCHTOWER

Here is a watchtower on which eight sentinels are standing. How can this tower be divided into four identical zones, each guarded by two sentinels?

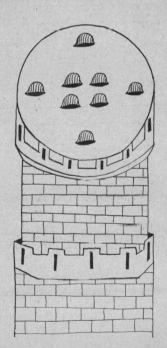

# VALON

Avalon is a square island surrounded by a river 4 yards wide. You have two boards 3.90 yards long and several inches wide. How can you arrange them to make a stable bridge allowing you to cross over to the legendary isle?

Solution on page 112

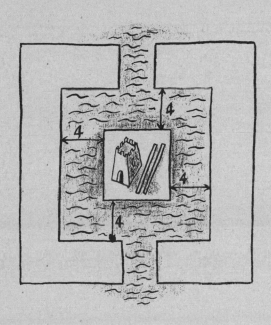

# AIN COURTYARD

This figure represents the paving of a main courtyard.
How many squares does it have in all?

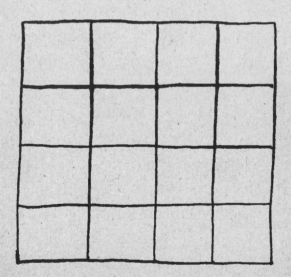

 EAPFROG

What is the minimum number of moves required by the demon to reverse the order of the pieces (so that the black ones are on the right and the white ones are on the left), given that:
- a piece can advance one space only,
- one piece can leap over another if it lands on an empty space.

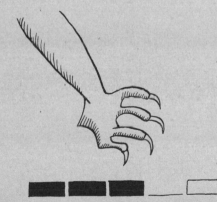

IRD BECOMES DRAGON

|   | 5 | 6 | 7 | 8 |
|---|---|---|---|---|
| 1 |   |   |   |   |
| 2 |   |   |   |   |
| 3 |   |   |   |   |
| 4 |   |   |   |   |

Solution on page 115

Study this enclosure holding both birds and dragons. Knowing that if you open locks 5, 6, 7 and 8, the animals in the corresponding column will permutate (the birds becoming dragons, and vice versa), and that the same will occur in the corresponding rows if you open locks 1, 2, 3 and 4, how many times do you need to open locks in order to change all the birds in the enclosure into dragons?

# ᴘOWER OF COINS

Place fifteen coins in five stacks of three coins arranged in a circle. After nine manoeuvres, you must end up with an increasing number of coins in successive stacks (one coin in stack A, two coins in stack B... five coins in stack E).

Each manoeuvre consists in distributing all of the coins from any stack at the start, placing one coin in each of the other stacks (even if empty) in clockwise order from the stack you've selected. When all of the coins in that stack have been distributed, you can then pick any other stack. What are the nine manoeuvres involved?

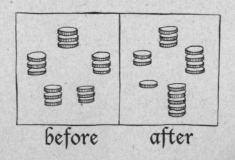

before          after

Solution on page 116

# ATHER AND SON

If you add the year of birth of a father, that of his son, the age of the father, and the age of the son, what result to do you obtain?

Solution on page 117

 ITTLE RECTANGLE
BECOMES SQUARE

Here is a rectangular parchment whose length (L = 2) is
twice its width (w = 1)

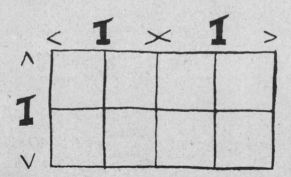

(In the diagram, the scale is 1 : 2)

How can you cut up this parchment in order to make a
square with the same surface area, using the pieces?

Solution on page 118

# ILLS

Lady Fredegonde's apothecary prescribes eight pills, to be taken one at a time every quarter of an hour. How much time will have passed by the time she finishes taking her pills?

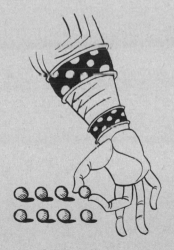

Solution on page 119

 OSEBUSH

Sister Blanche plants a rosebush in the gardens of Fontevrault abbey. To another nun who enquires about the size of the rosebush, she replies:
'It measures 30 inches, plus half its own height.'

How tall is the rosebush?

Solution on page 120

 ANDICAPS

You are blind, deaf and dumb. How many senses do you still possess?

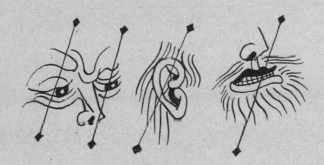

UCKY DRAW

A tyrannical king has captured his most bitter opponent.
The next day, he gives the man a last chance to be pardoned.
He places two marbles in a helmet, one white symbolising
freedom, and one black representing death.

In front of the people gathered for the occasion, the prisoner
must draw unseen a single marble which will decide his fate.

The night before, a spy informs the prisoner that the king
has placed two black marbles in the helmet.

What should he do to ensure that he will be set free, after
drawing a single marble?

# HERE IS THE FATHER?

Lady Bertha is twenty-one years older than her son. In six years, he will be one-fifth of his mother's age.

Question:
Where is the father?

Solution on page 123

 HEEP

An old shepherd declares to his wife:

'When I die, I want our eldest son to receive half my sheep, our middle son to receive a third, and our youngest son a ninth. At the moment of his passing, the shepherd has seventeen sheep. After wracking their brains, his three sons fail to see any way to respect the will of their father, without carving up the sheep.

Eventually, another old shepherd, a friend of their father, finds the solution to their problem.

What does he propose?

Solution on page 124

# O YOUR QUILLS

Draw this figure without lifting your pencil from the paper or passing twice through the same spot.

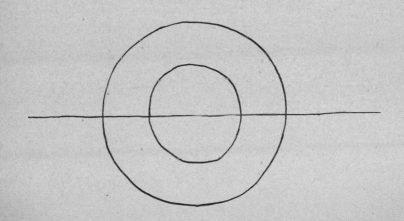

Solution on page 125

# ADDITION

How can you obtain 1,000 from a numerical addition containing only 8s?

Solution on page 126

# AGNETISM

You have two iron cylinders 6 inches long, with a base ½ inch in diameter. These two cylinders are identical in all respects, except that one is magnetized at both ends and the other is not. If you are in a locked room whose sole piece of furniture is a wooden table and without any other metallic object except for these two cylinders, how can you determine which of the two cylinders is magnetized?

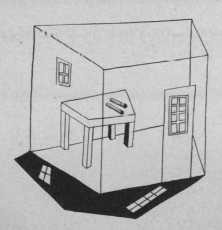

Solution on page 127

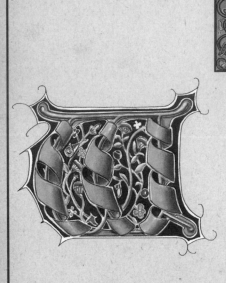

# WINE LEVEL

Two drunkards find a cask of wine without a lid, perfectly symmetrical, and roughly half full of wine. One of the men asserts that the level of wine is actually more than half of the cask, while the other claims that it is less.

How can they determine which of them is right, knowing that they have neither a measuring instrument of any sort, nor any container?

Solution on page 128

# ATCHES

The master glazier is planning the composition of his stained glass window with the help of some matches. His problem is the following: how can he obtain three squares from this drawing by removing eight matches?

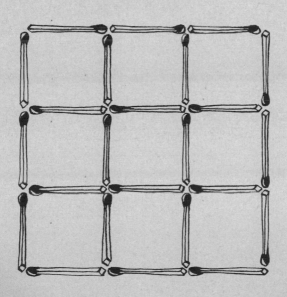

# SYMBOLS

| | | | | | | | |
|---|---|---|---|---|---|---|---|
| | a | 2 | a | | | | |
| | e | | g | e | | | |
| | 8 | | g | | h | | 8 |
| 2 | | | h | | 3 | 3 | |
| 8 | h | | | 2 | e | e | |
| | | a | g | | | | 2 |
| | | 3 | h | g | 3 | | |
| | | a | | | 8 | | |

Divide this square into four parts equal in size and in such a way that each part contains seven different symbols.

Solution on page 130

# LOGICAL SERIES 3

Continue this series:

1 (2,3) 2 (5,6) 4 (11,30) 26 (?,?) ?

Solution on page 131

# WO RESULTS FOR THE SAME NUMBER?

Let a = 0.99999999999999999... (to infinity)
Note: there is a number with infinite decimal places - think of the famous $\sqrt{2}$.
So let us take a, the number whose integral part is 0 and whose decimal part is an infinite series of 9s.

a = 0.99999999999999... [1] By definition.
10 × a = 9.99999999999999... [2] Multiply by 10.
10 × a = 9 + 0.9999999999999... [3]
Separate the integral and decimal parts on the right side of the equation.
10 × a = 9 + a [4] By definition.
10 × a - a = 9 [5]. Subtract a from both sides.
9 × a = 9 [6] Using the fact that 10 - 1 = 9.
a = 1 [7] Divide both sides by 9.

Question: Is it then true that 1 = 0.99999999999999999... ?

Solution on page 132

# ALL IN THE HEAD

Do the following calculation in your head:

The initial amount is 1 million.
Divide it by 4.
Divide the result by 5.
Divide the result by 2.
Divide the result by 20.
Subtract 50.
Divide by 3 then by 8.
Subtract 1.
Divide the result by 7.
Add 2.
Divide by 3.
Add 2.
Lastly, divide by 5.

What result do you obtain?

Solution on page 133

 HIELD TRIANGLES

Have a look at these two shields:

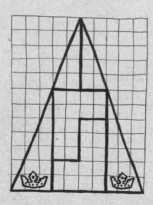 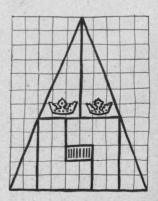

Solution on page 134

The parts of the first shield have been rearranged to form the second, to which two small squares have had to be added. How do you explain the presence of these squares, shown as a striped rectangle?

Hint 1
Certain points, which seem to be aligned, are not, in fact.

Hint 2
The two shields are not triangles.

PHINX

What animal has four feet in the morning, two at noon, and three in the evening?

Solution on page 135

# ECHANICAL ALARM CLOCK

You need to wake up early tomorrow morning so you use your mechanical alarm clock (with hour and minute hands) because it has a loud ring. You set it to ring at 10am and you go to sleep at 9pm.

How long will you sleep?

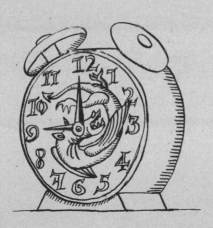

# PURSES

How can you alternate purses full of coins and empty purses by only touching a single purse?

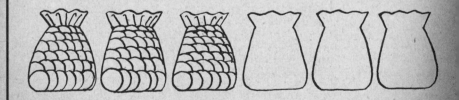

Solution on page 137

# ULE DRIVER

A mule tender is about to enter a lane with a sign reading, 'Mules Forbidden.'

He looks at the sign without grumbling and starts up the lane before being stopped by a soldier of the local constabulary.

The two converse for a moment and the mule driver continues unhindered.

How is this possible?

Solution on page 138

# PRISON

Seven prisoners are locked up in a tower of the royal castle. To prevent them killing one another, the provost decides to separate them by erecting three walls. How should these walls be placed, if the size of each cell is of no importance?

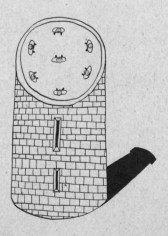

Solution on page 139

# ELEVEN BRANCHES

Two knights are contending for the hand of a lady at the royal court. To settle the matter, the king brings them before a table on which he has placed eleven branches.

Each of them in turn has the right to take away one, two, or three branches. The king decides that the knight who ends up taking the last branch shall renounce his claim.

Knowing that he will go first, how many branches should Gawain take in order to be sure of winning?

Solution on page 140

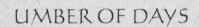

# NUMBER OF DAYS

Certain months have thirty-one days and others only have thirty.

How many months had twenty-eight days between January 1008 and December 1012?

Solution on page 141

# PADLOCK

As a token of her love, Isolde wishes to send Tristan a casket containing locks of her hair. So that no one else can open this incriminating box, Tristan and Isolde each possess a padlock that will secure the casket.

However, in order to avoid discovery, neither of the two lovers can have the padlock key belonging to the other.

How should the lovers proceed so when Tristan receives the sealed casket he is able to open it?

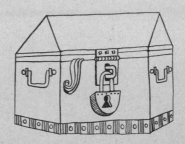

Solution on page 142

 ASUALTIES OF WAR

If 70% of soldiers have lost their eye during the course of a battle, 75% an ear, 80% an arm, and 85% a leg, what is the minimum percentage that have lost an eye, an ear, an arm, and a leg, all in this same battle?

Solution on page 143

# WO GUARDS

A prisoner is locked up in a tower which has two doors. One of them leads to the exit, the other to the dungeon. A guard is placed before each door. One of them always tells the truth, the other always lies.

What single question can the prisoner ask of just one of these two guards to be sure of finding the door that leads to freedom?

Solution on page 144

# REVERSIBLE TRIANGLE

An archer lets fly a series of arrows forming a triangle whose point is on the left. How can you obtain a similar triangle, but with the point on the right, by moving just three arrows?

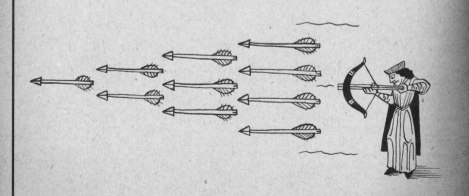

Solution on page 145

# UNIVERSITY

At the University, a master poses a problem to the young clerics he teaches:

1. It's better than God.
2. It's worse than the Devil.
3. The poor have it.
4. The rich need it.
5. And if you eat it, you die.

What is it?

GOD

DEVIL

Solution on page 146

# UINEVERE

To punish Guinevere for her infidelity, King Arthur locks her up in one of the impregnable round towers of his castle.

Full of sorrow, the queen, starting from the door, which is not facing due south, first walks towards the north of the tower over a distance of 30 paces before bumping into the wall. She then decides to go in a straight line west and runs into the wall again after 40 paces.

What is the diameter of the tower?

Solution on page 147

 ARPET

Charlemagne's bedchamber measures 12 by 9 yards.
In the middle is a rectangular fireplace 8 yards long and 1 yard
wide. The chamber thus has a usable surface of 100 square
yards (12 x 9 - 8 x 1) = 100). It is represented by the figure
below:

To make it more comfortable,
the Emperor wants to cover
the floor with a carpet brought
from the Orient, measuring 10
x 10 yds.

How can the entire floor
be covered with this carpet,
by cutting it into two
superimposable pieces of the
same size?

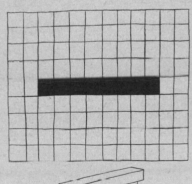

 ENS' EGGS

Eight hundred hens lay on average eight hundred eggs in eight days.

How many eggs do four hundred hens lay in four days?

Solution on page 149

 OGICAL SERIES 4

Complete this series:

1 3 5 4 4 4...

# ENTAL CALCULATION

Divide 30 by ½ then add 20 to the result.
What number do you get?

# ATCH SQUARE

Four matches are arranged in a cross:

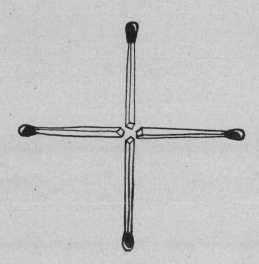

How can you obtain a square by moving just a single match?

 HESTS

Some brigands are interrupted as they are robbing the king's treasury. They manage to carry off three chests, but they don't have the keys.

One of the chests contains gold coins, another silver, while the third has both gold and silver coins.

Each chest originally had a label indicating its contents, but during their flight, the brigands have mixed them up and all three labels are now attached to the wrong chests.

They can only spy one coin through the keyhole of each chest.

Into which chest should they look in order to know right away what each chest contains?

Solution on page 153

# RECIOUS STONES

King Louis the Large wants to have a crown made with precious stones. He knows from an informer that one of the nine stones presented to him by the merchant is a fake. But the merchant won't admit to this. The king also knows that each of the stones weighs the same, except the fake, which is slightly heavier. So, he asks the merchant to bring out his scales and manages to find the false stone with just two weighings.

How does he manage this?

Solution on page 154

 HADOW OF THE
TOWER

In the shadow of the tower, strange phenomena occur...
What difference do you see between square A and square B?

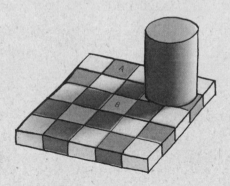

Solution on page 155

# INE POINTS

Let's assume we have a grid of nine points that looks like this:

Looking at his plan, the architect of the crypt wonders how he can connect these points by drawing four straight lines without lifting his pen... Can you help him?

Solution on page 156

 LIMBING SNAIL

A snail wants to climb to the top of a wall that is 10yds high.

But it moves in a very particular fashion: during the course of the day it climbs 3yds, and during the night, it descends 2yds.

If it starts its ascent one morning, how many days will it require to reach the top of this wall?

Hint:
10 days is not the correct answer.

Solution on page 157

# IVE TRIANGLES

An alchemist wants to move four matches to form five triangles. How should he do this?

Solution on page 158

# OWER TRANSFER

You need to transfer, one by one, all of the segments of the tower to the empty space on the right without ever placing a bigger segment on top of a smaller one, in a maximum of fifteen moves.

You can use the space in the middle as a transit point.

Solution on page 159

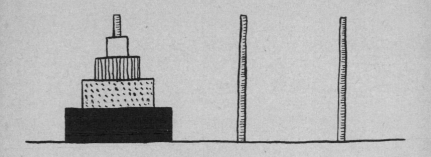

# OUR QUEENS AND A BISHOP

On a chessboard, how can four queens and a bishop be placed so that the opposing king is always in check, whatever his position?

Reminder: queens can move in straight lines or diagonally, bishops move diagonally.

|   | a | b | c | d | e | f | g | h |
|---|---|---|---|---|---|---|---|---|
| 8 |   |   |   |   |   |   |   |   |
| 7 |   |   |   |   |   |   |   |   |
| 6 |   |   |   |   |   |   |   |   |
| 5 |   |   |   |   |   |   |   |   |
| 4 |   |   |   |   |   |   |   |   |
| 3 |   |   |   |   |   |   |   |   |
| 2 |   |   |   |   |   |   |   |   |
| 1 |   |   |   |   |   |   |   |   |

Solution on page 160

# Solutions

RAIN-TEASER

| a | b | c | d | e |
| c | d | e | a | b |
| e | a | b | c | d |
| b | c | d | e | a |
| d | e | a | b | c |

Solution for page 10

# AKE 24 WITH 5, 5, 5 AND 1

$1 \div 5 = 0.2$

$5 - 0.2 = 4.8$

$4.8 \times 5 - 24$

Who said the numbers had to be whole ones?

Once again, we observe the natural tendency of the human mind to add unnecessary constraints when tackling problems...

 OGICAL SERIES 1

The terms of this series correspond to the initials of the numbers:
'One, Two, Three, Four, Five, Six, Seven, Eight, Nine, Ten...'

o t t f f s s 8 9 10
1 2 3 4 5 6 7 e n t

 EAR

The circles seem to turn.
Don't you think that's odd?

OGICAL SERIES 2

The terms of this series correspond to the last letters of the numbers onE twO threE fouR fivE siX seveN eighT...

# ...N T...

Solution for page 16

# UBTRACTION

Just once.

   After that, you're subtracting from 30, no longer from 36!

Solution for page 17

# RAGONFLY

The lovers, advancing at the same speed, each travel 50 furlongs at a speed of 10 furlongs per hour. They therefore meet at the end of 5 hours.

So, the dragonfly will have flown:

$5 \times 150 = 750$ furlongs.

750

# P

ATHS

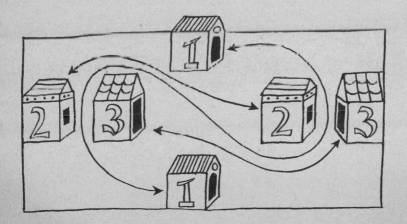

# 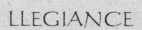LLEGIANCE

There are only three combinations of truth and falsehood, shown below. Only the third combination is possible and therefore both are lying, which means that Sir Thomas serves King Richard and Sir Robert serves Prince John.

| If... | | Then... | | Possible |
|---|---|---|---|---|
| Sir Thomas says | Sir Robert says | Sir Thomas serves | Sir Robert serves | |
| True | False | Prince John | Prince John | No |
| False | True | King Richard | King Richard | No |
| False | False | King Richard | Prince John | Yes |

EHIND BARS

The prisoner, like most people, sees grey points between the squares. Yet they don't exist! Strange, isn't it?

# NKWELL

Let x be the cost of the quill.

The cost of the inkwell equals $x + 10$

The sum of the two objects equals $x + x + 10 = 11$

Therefore $2x + 10 = 11$

$2x = 11 - 10 = 1$

$x = 1 \div 2 = 0.5$

The quill thus costs half a shilling and the inkwell ten and a half shillings.

# OOL STOCKINGS

Since there three different colours, by taking four wool stockings from her chest, Lady Brunehaut can be sure of having a matched pair.

#  ASTIME

He turns over the two hourglasses, until the little one is empty, at 4 minutes.

He turns over the little one and lets it run down until the big one is empty, at 7 minutes.

He turns over the big one and lets it run down until the little one is empty. 8 minutes have gone by.

Lastly, he turns over the big one and waits for it to empty. He can then take his sauce off the fire, because the 9 minutes are up.

Solution for page 24

# T THE MARKET

Let us assume that:

$x$ = the amount that Lady Ermangarde had upon entering a shop.

$y$ = the amount she had upon leaving the same shop.

The amount she spent $(x - y)$ in the shop is therefore $x \div 2 + 10$, this can be expressed as

$$x - y = (x \div 2 + 10)$$
$$x - x \div 2 - 10 = y$$
$$x \div 2 - 10 = y$$
$$x \div 2 = y + 10$$
$$x = 2 \times (y + 10)$$

This equation can be applied in each shop.

After the last shop, she has nothing left; so we can posit that $y = 0$:

$$2 \times (0 + 10) = 20$$

She thus had 20 shillings upon entering the last shop.

The same calculation applied to the preceding shops gives us:

$$2 \times (20 + 10) = 60$$
$$2 \times (60 + 10) = 140$$
$$2 \times (140 + 10) = 300$$
$$2 \times (300 + 10) = 620$$

She had 620 shillings at the start.

# ALINDROME

The next palindrome is 16061.

The knight thus travels 110 furlongs in 2 hours, which means that he rides at a speed of 55 furlongs per hour.

# RIDGE CROSSING

First of all, A and B cross, which takes 2 minutes.

Then A brings back the torch, and 3 minutes have gone by.

C and D cross the bridge, and now 13 minutes have been used up.

B returns with the torch, and we're now at 15 minutes.

A and B cross the bridge, and 17 minutes have elapsed since the start. Quick, the ghoul is coming back!

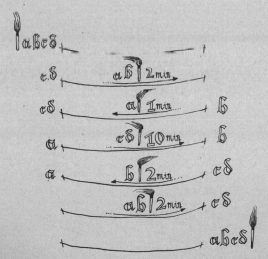

Solution for page 28

 ALL

All he needs to do is wait for it to rain. Once the rainwater has filled the bucket he can pour it into the hole and the liquid will force the ball to rise up and out of the hole.

Solution for page 30

# 29 FEBRUARY

He will be 28 years old.

  Every year the same date in the same month will fall a day later in the week, because 365 is a multiple of 7 plus 1.

In leap years, which have 366 days, it falls two days later.

Leap years occur every four years.

Between two February 29s, there is therefore a difference of five days (3 + 2).

So the first 29 February after the birth of a child will fall five days later, on a Saturday.

  The second will fall on a Thursday, third on a Tuesday, the fourth on a Sunday, the fifth on a Friday, the sixth on a Wednesday, and finally the seventh on a Monday.

  Lady Gertrude's son will thus be $7 \times 4 = 28$ years old the next time his birthday falls on a Monday.

# PARALLELEPIPED

No! AB = BC
Curious, isn't it?

Solution for page 32

# ONG RECTANGLE BECOMES SQUARE

The area of the rectangle formed by the parchment is 5 (w × L = 5 × 1 = 1). Therefore the side of the square must be √5.

So the parchment is cut up in a way to make the straight segments with a length of √5 appear:

They can be rearranged like this:

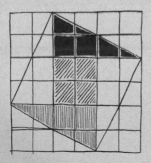

And the long rectangle is transformed into a square!

 YCLING RACE

Roland finishes fourth. By passing the rider in second place, he puts himself in second (and not in first). So when the two other competitors pass him, he falls back into fourth position.

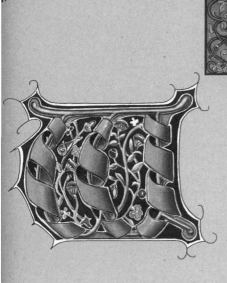 ATCHTOWER

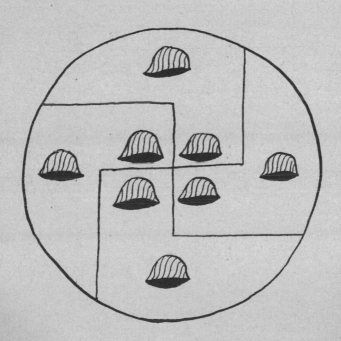

# AVALON

Here's how to do it:

Solution for page 36

# AIN COURTYARD

The figure representing the main courtyard is composed of thirty squares:

- sixteen of size 1 × 1;
- nine of size 2 × 2;
- four of size 3 × 3;
- and one of size 4 × 4.

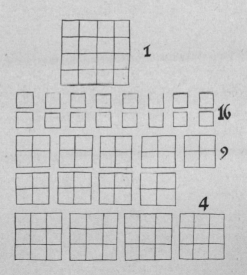

 EAPFROG

You need a minimum of fifteen moves to reverse the order of the pieces in this configuration.

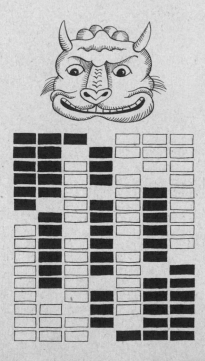

Solution for page 39

IRD BECOMES
DRAGON

It is possible to convert all of the birds in the enclosure into dragons in just four steps:

### Step 1 - Open lock 2

### Step 4 - Open lock 4.

### Steps 2 and 3 -
### Open locks 5 and 8.

# OWER OF COINS

Label the five stacks as A, B, C, D, and E.
The nine successive manoeuvres should
start, in order, from the following stacks: A,
B, C, D, E, D, C, B, A.

 ATHER AND SON

A figure double that of the curent year.

# ITTLE RECTANGLE BECOMES SQUARE

The area of the rectangular parchment is 2 (I x L = 2 x 1 = 2). Therefore each side of the square must be the root of 2.

   The parchment is therefore cut so that we get four segments whose longest side is root 2.

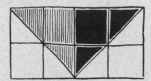

They are rearranged like this:

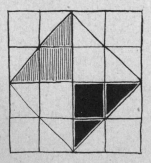

And the rectangle becomes a square!

Solution for page 44

ILLS

1 hr 45 min will have passed.

# ROSEBUSH

The rose bush measures 60 ins (30 ins + half of 60 ins, or 30 ins).

60

Solution for page 46

# ANDICAPS

You still have three senses remaining. For those who answered two, remember that speech is not a sense!

# LUCKY DRAW

The prisoner needs to draw one of the marbles at random
and swallow it without looking at it. Then, the only way of
knowing which marble he drew will be to look at the marble
remaining in the helmet, which will of course be black.

The king, in the presence of his people, will have to resign
himself to freeing the prisoner.

Solution for page 48

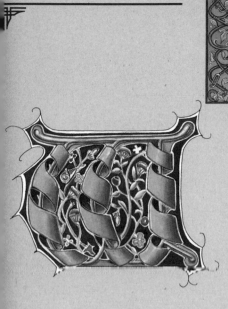

# HERE IS THE FATHER?

Let $x$ be the age in years of the son and let $y$ be the age in years of his mother, Lady Bertha.

Lady Bertha is twenty-one years older than her son. So we can assume that: $x + 21 = y$.

In six years, he will be one-fifth of his mother's age. So we can assume that: $5 \times (x + 6) = y + 6$

Frome this equation we derive:

$5x + 6 = y + 6$

$y = 5x + 24$

We replace y in the first equation:

$x + 21 = 5x + 24$

$-3 = 4x$

$x = -3 \div 4 \text{ years} = -9 \text{ months}$

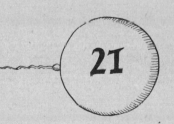

So the father must be very close to the mother!

 HEEP

The old shepherd lends a sheep to the three sons, which brings the number of sheep to eighteen.

Respecting the will of his old friend, he gives half to the eldest son, or nine sheep, a third to the middle son, six sheep, and a ninth to the last son, or two sheep.

This makes a total of $9 + 6 + 2 = 17$ sheep.

The terms of the will have been respected, and the old man can retrieve his sheep.

# O YOUR QUILLS

You must trace the following path:
- from A to B,
- then the upper curve to E,
- then go to D,
- then the upper curve to C,
- then the straight line to D,
- then the lower curve to C,
- then the straight line to B,
- then the lower curve to E,
- then the straight line to F.

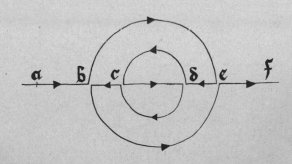

# ADDITION

$$8 + 8 + 8 + 88 + 888 = 1000$$

Solution for page 52

# AGNETISM

You should place them in the form of a T.

If nothing happens, the magnet is the one forming the horizontal bar of the T.

If they attract or repel, the magnet is the one constituting the T's vertical bar.

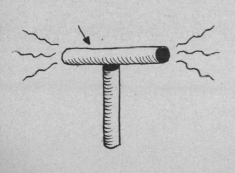

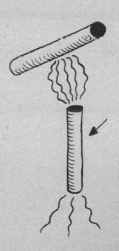

# ᴡINE LEVEL

The men must lean the cask over until the wine comes right up to the brim, and then examine the bottom of the cask.

If they cannot see the bottom because it is covered by wine, then the cask is more than half-full.

If they can see any part of the bottom of the cask, then it is less than half-full.

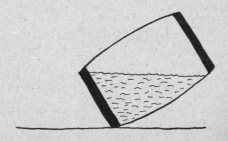

Solution for page 54

# ATCHES 1

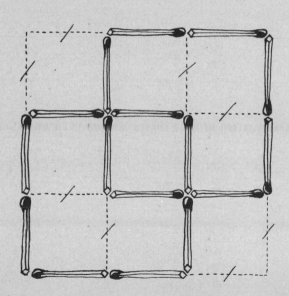

YMBOLS

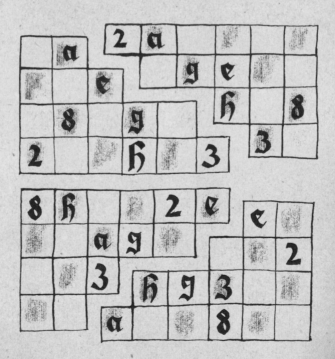

 OGICAL SERIES 3

1 (2,3) 2 (5,6) 4 (11,30) 26 (41,330) 304

The number in front of a parenthesis is the difference between the second number of the preceding parenthesis and the number in front of that parenthesis.

Example: $2 = 3 - 1$

The first number of each parenthesis is equal to the sum of the two numbers in the preceding parenthesis.

Example: $11 = 5 + 6$

The second number of each parenthesis is equal to the product of the two numbers in the preceding parenthesis

Example: $30 = 5 \times 6$

The three numbers that continue the series are therefore (41,330) 304:

$11 + 30 = 41$

$11 \times 30 = 330$

$330 - 26 = 304$

Solution for page 57

# WO RESULTS FOR THE SAME NUMBER?

The answer to the question is yes!
It is true that $1 = 0.9999999999999...$
And this calculation is proof of that.

Note: between lines 3 and 4, you need to remind yourself that infinity - 1 is still infinity.

Another (but less elegant) demonstration:

$$1 = 3 \times (1 \div 3) = 3 \times 0.3333333... = 0.9999999...$$

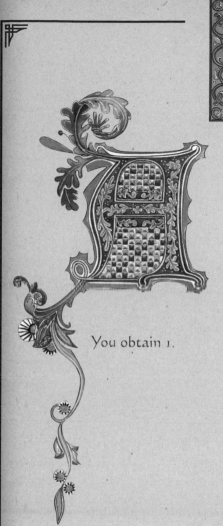

# ALL IN THE HEAD

You obtain 1.

# HIELD TRIANGLES

The two shields are not actually triangles. Look closely at points A, D, and G: they are not aligned.

In fact, the slope of the hypotenuse of triangle ADB is different from that of triangle DGE: point D would be slightly to the right of the straight line AG if we took the trouble to draw it. And similarly in the case of point F. From this fact it follows that figure ACFGD has a surface area that is less than an imaginary triangle ACG. In the same way, on the second shield, points HJL and IKL are not aligned: points J and K are outside of a triangle HIL. From the fact that the first shield has a surface area that is less than a 'true' triangle, it follows that there is a difference in area between the two.

In the last diagram, the two shields are superimposed. If they formed triangles, the surface AJGD would have an area of zero.

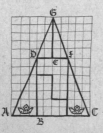 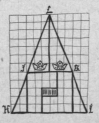 

Solution for page 60

 PHINX

Man: in his infancy, he walks on all fours, as an adult, he stands up on two legs, and lastly, in his old age, he moves about with the help of a cane.

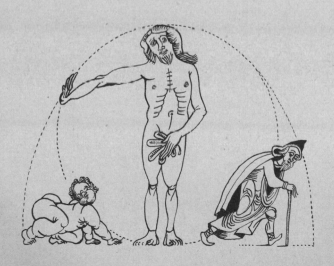

Solution for page 62

# ECHANICAL
# ALARM CLOCK

You will sleep for an hour.

A clock with hands does not differentiate between 10am and 10pm. So it will go off at 10pm.

Solution for page 63

# PURSES

You need to empty the contents of the second purse into the fifth and then replace the second, now empty, back in its original spot.

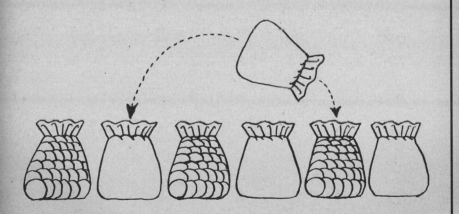

# ULE DRIVER

He's on foot and doesn't have his mule with him.

RISON

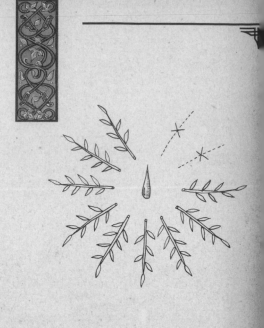

# ELEVEN BRANCHES

The solution is twofold:

Gawain takes two branches. The other knight can take one, two or three branches. In all these cases, Gawain will take three, two, or one branches, so as to collect the sixth (there will then remain five on the table).

From that point, when his rival takes one, two, or three branches, Gawain will gather up three, two, or one respectively, thus leaving the last one to the other knight.

# NUMBER OF DAYS

From January 1008 to December 1012, five years have gone by, that is, $5 \times 12 = 60$ months.
 During this period, there are sixty months with twenty-eight days, since every month has at least twenty-eight days!

# ADLOCK

After having placed the locks of her hair in the box, Isolde must secure it with her padlock and send it to Tristan. Upon receiving the box, he will add his own padlock and send it back to her.

Isolde receives the box, removes the padlock belonging to her, and sends it once again to her lover, who upon receipt can now remove his padlock and find the celebrated love token.

Solution for page 69

 ASUALTIES OF WAR

30% have both eyes,
25% have both ears,
20% have both arms
and 15% have two legs.
So at least 90% are not suffering from all four handicaps.
That makes a minimum of 10% who are missing an eye, an ear,
an arm, and a leg all at the same time.

Solution for page 70

# TWO GUARDS

He must ask one of the two guards:

'Which door will the other guard tell me is the door leading to the exit?'

Then all he has to do is to choose the opposite door.

# REVERSIBLE TRIANGLE

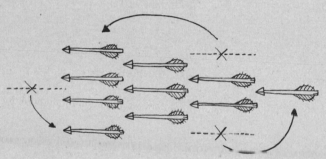

NIVERSITY

The answer is 'nothing.'
Nothing is better than God.
Nothing is worse than the Devil.
The poor have nothing.
The rich need nothing.
And if you eat nothing, you die.

NOTHING

Solution for page 73

# UINEVERE

Starting from any point on the circumference of the tower, the queen first of all headed north until she reached another point on the tower's circumference. Then she turned 90° to the west until she ran into the wall again.

Her trajectory corresponds to the two shorter sides of a right-angled triangle, measuring respectively 30 and 40 paces. Now, the hypotenuse of a right-angled triangle inscribed in a circle coincides with its diameter.

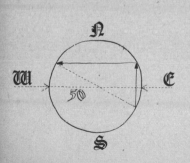

Knowing that the square of the hypotenuse of a right-angled triangle is equal to the sum of the squares of the other two sides, we have:

$$\text{hypotenuse}^2 = 30^2 + 40^2$$
$$\text{hypotenuse}^2 = 900 + 1600 = 2500$$
$$\text{hypotenuse} = \sqrt{2500} = 50$$

The tower has a diameter of 50 paces.

ARPET

Here is the cut that needs to be made in the carpet:

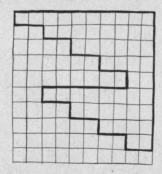

And this is how the entire chamber is covered:

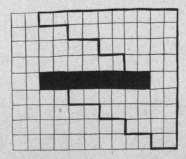

 ENS' EGGS

Two hundred eggs.

In fact, four hundred hens lay four hundred eggs in eight days. Therefore four hundred hens lay two hundred eggs in four days.

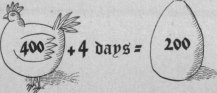

Solution for page 76

OGICAL SERIES 4

Each term in this series corresponds to the number of letters comprising the name of the preceding number ('five' has four letters, 'four' has four letters...)

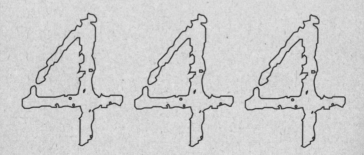

# ENTAL CALCULATION

Unless you've made a mistake, you
should have 80.

Because $30 \div (1 \div 2) = 30 \times 2 = 60$
$60 + 20 = 80$.

# ATCH SQUARE

You need to take square in its arithmetic sense rather than the geometric one.

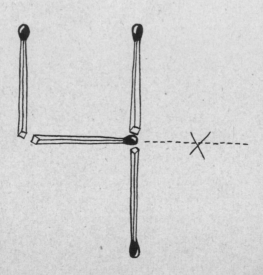

 HESTS

The bandits only need to glance into the chest bearing the label: 'gold and silver coins.' Indeed, since none of the labels are in their right place, this means that:
  - if they see a gold coin, this chest can only contain gold coins,
  - if they see a silver coin, this chest can only contain silver coins.
  From this, they can deduce the contents of the two other chests.

Solution for page 80

# PRECIOUS STONES

1a. The king chooses at random three stones for the left-hand tray, and three for the right-hand one. If the trays are balanced, the fake is one of the other three stones (let us call them the 'heavier three') and he proceeds to step 2a.

1b. If, on the other hand, one tray weighs more, the king knows the fake stone is among these three; he then proceeds to step 2a with the 'heavier three'.

2a. The king chooses a stone at random from the 'heavier three' for the left-hand tray and another stone for the right-hand one. If the trays are balanced, he can deduce from this that the fake stone is the third in the trio.

2b. If, however, one tray weighs more, that means the fake stone is sitting upon it.

 HADOW OF THE TOWER

None; square A is the same shade as square B. Perplexing, isn't it?

Solution for page 82

# NINE POINTS

Here's one way of doing this:

Nobody said you couldn't go outside the framework formed by the eight points…

 LIMBING SNAIL

It reaches the top of the wall on the evening of the eighth day:

Yards

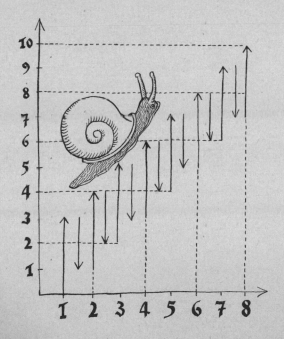

Solution for page 84

# IVE TRIANGLES

We get: 1 big triangle + 4 small triangles = 5 triangles.

Solution for page 85

# POWER TRANSFER

| | | |
|---|---|---|
| 1234 | | |
| 234 | 1 | |
| 34 | 1 | 2 |
| 34 | | 12 |
| 4 | 3 | 12 |
| 14 | 3 | 2 |
| 14 | 23 | |
| 4 | 123 | |
| | 123 | 4 |
| | 23 | 14 |
| 2 | 3 | 14 |
| 12 | 3 | 4 |
| 12 | | 34 |
| 2 | 1 | 34 |
| | 1 | 234 |
| | | 1234 |

Solution for page 86

# OUR QUEENS AND A BISHOP

One possible solution is to place the queens on C5, D3, E4, and H8, and lastly the bishop on A2.